Chefs' Special

Parsi Kitchen

Chefs' Special

Parsi Kitchen

Jeani Mohindra

Lustre Press
Roli Books

Acknowledgements

I would like to begin by offering my sincere thanks to my friend, Usha Gopinathan, who approached me with the idea of writing on Parsi cuisine and continuously lent her encouragement.

This book would not have been possible if it was not for the tremendous moral support and encouragement given by my husband, Vinay Mohindra, and the efforts of my darling daughter, Suparna, who tirelessly typed the entire text and constantly provided much-needed enthusiasm and help with the choice of recipes. My long-distance source of inspiration has been my son, Rohit, daughter-in-law, Sangeeta, and my little grandson, Shiv, all the way from New York.

I am also grateful to my loving sisters Roda Soonawalla and Zarine Chothia, both great chefs. Over the years, we have created, shared and perfected many of our special family recipes.

Lastly, I am thankful for being part of two good, food-loving communities (Parsi and Punjabi) as I have always enjoyed cooking for my family and have been constantly motivated by their appreciation.

Flavours of Parsi Cooking

The history of the Zoroastrian Parsees or Parsis, followers of the ancient Persian religion known as Zoroastrianism, goes back over 1,300 years to the dawn of civilisation. The followers of Zarathustra, they claim Aryas vaegah (the cradle of the Aryans) as their first primitive home. Fire, their scared symbol, was discovered by one of their earliest known kings, Haoshyangha of the Pishadadian period. Parsis are a thriving, peace loving, jovial and cohesive community spread all over the globe.

Parsi food is the amalgamation of all the varied techniques found in the Middle East and Asia. They married their styles of cooking meats, eggs and seafood with the spices of this land. They maintained all their traditions, but also developed a cuisine that has piqued the interest of all Indians. It is just as rich, spicy and varied as any other Indian regional cooking genre. It is unique in its own way, using ingredients from all over the world and assimilating the influences that have shaped the history of its community. Parsis prefer non-vegetarian food, mainly consisting of fish, lamb and chicken, and limited vegetarian dishes. Parsi curry is a typical example of the combination of influences of Iran (nuts), Gujarat and Maharashtra (coconut and spices). Coconut, fish, and rice are considered symbols of plenty and no Parsi feast is complete without these items.

Food plays a very important role in all Parsi festivals; certain foods are traditionally cooked and eaten on special occasions like birthdays, *navjote* (thread ceremony), and weddings. *Dhan Dar* (split red gram tempered with garlic) served with rice always makes its appearance on birthdays and other auspicious occasions. Fish, too, is served on these occasions. In fact, so auspicious is fish that a sweet made with dry fruits, dispensed on occasions like engagements and new years, is fashioned in the shape of a fish. *Rava* (semolina garnished with dried fruits) and *sev* (dry vermicelli delight) are also traditionally served on auspicious occasions.

Parsis have never been bothered by any finicky restrictions on food, and have never touted abstinence as a virtue. Meat is an important part of Parsi cuisine, particularly lamb. Pork was not much favoured in the old days and beef, in deference to Hindu neighbours, was also not indulged in much. Meat is cooked, curiously enough, with a variety of vegetables. Example, *papeta ma gosht* (lamb with potatoes). It is also cooked with a variety of dals as in *kala masoor dal ma gosht* (lamb in a thick lentil gravy) and the celebrated *dhansak* (lamb cooked with mixed pulses and vegetables). A variety of dals are used in Parsi cooking, doubtless a borrowing from Gujarati cooking.

Jamva chalo ji (let's go for dinner) . . . the words fall like music on the ears of all Parsis on wedding feasts. Guests sit at rows of tables covered with crisp, white cloth and dinner is served on banana leaves. From here the Parsi food journey commences in full earnest and can last for 45 minutes to as much as an hour, spread over various courses.

As you discover the various dishes described in this book, you will find a unique blend of spices that make Parsi food very appetising, nutritious and wholesome.

Basic Preparations

Dhansak Masala

Take 1 kg coriander (*dhaniya*) seeds, 250 gm cumin (*jeera*) seeds, 1″ piece turmeric (*haldi*), 50 gm cinnamon (*dalchini*) sticks, 50 gm cloves (*laung*), 200 gm black peppercorns (*sabut kali mirch*), 50 gm white cardamoms (*safed elaichi*), 50 gm mustard seeds (*rai*), 50 gm poppy seeds (*khuskhus*), 50 gm curry leaves (*kadhi patta*), 60 gm black cumin seeds (*shah jeera*), 50 gm fenugreek seeds (*methi dana*), 50 gm bay leaves (*tej patta*), 50 gm dried orange peel (pith should be removed), and 50 gm dried sweet lime peel (pith should be removed).

Roast each ingredient individually with just 1-2 tsp oil on a griddle (*tawa*). Cool, grind and mix. Store in an airtight glass container. This can be kept for over a year.

Curry Powder

Take 400 gm coriander (*dhaniya*) seeds, 200 gm cumin (*jeera*) seeds, 100 gm fenugreek seeds (*methi dana*), 75 gm dry red chillies (mixture of Kashmiri, Goan and local chillies is preferable), 50 gm turmeric (*haldi*) powder, 75 gm dry ginger powder (*sonth*), 75 gm dry garlic powder, 19 gm bay leaves (*tej patta*), 10 gm curry leaves (*kadhi patta*), 75 gm mustard seeds (*rai*), 100 gm poppy seeds (*khuskhus*), 250 gm roasted gram, 50 gm black sesame seeds (*til*), 5 gm cinnamon (*dalchini*) sticks, 5 gm cloves (*laung*), 5 gm white cardamoms (*safed elaichi*), weighed and peeled, 10 gm black peppercorns (*sabut kali mirch*), 2 nutmegs (*jaiphal*), 5 gm salt, and 2 tbsp vegetable oil.

Wash and dry the coriander seeds, cumin seeds, and fenugreek seeds individually. Dry roast and grind each ingredient individually and then mix them all together. Heat the oil till very hot, sprinkle onto the spices and mix well (this preserves the masala for a longer time). Store in an airtight glass container.

Parsi *Sambhar* Masala

Take 1 tbsp mustard oil, 2 gm asafoetida (*hing*), 125 gm garlic (*lasan*), ground, 250 gm dry red chillies (*sookhi lal mirch*), 125 gm cumin (*jeera*) powder, 125 gm mustard seeds (*rai*), coarsely ground, 125 gm salt, and 200 gm turmeric (*haldi*) powder.

In a big pan, heat the mustard oil. Add the asafoetida, then the remaining ingredients. Cook till a fragrant smell emanates. When cool, store in an airtight jar.

Papeta Na Sada Pattice

Deep-fried potato cakes

Preparation time: 30 min.
Cooking time: 25 min.
Makes: 20

Ingredients:

Potatoes, boiled, mashed	6
Carrots (*gajar*), boiled, mashed	3
Green peas (*matar*), boiled, mashed	1 cup
Turmeric (*haldi*) powder	½ tsp / 1 gm
Red chilli powder	1 tsp / 2 gm
Cumin (*jeera*) seeds, roasted, coarsely ground	1 tsp / 2 gm
Pickled green pepper, coarsely ground	1 tsp / 2 gm
Green coriander (*hara dhaniya*), freshly chopped	2 tbsp / 8 gm
Lemon (*nimbu*) juice	2 tbsp / 30 ml
Salt to taste	
Eggs, beaten	4-6
Breadcrumbs	2 cups / 240 gm
Vegetable oil	2 cups / 400 ml

Method:

1. Mix all the ingredients (except eggs, breadcrumbs and oil) together in a bowl.
2. With wet palms, divide the mixture equally into 20 portions. Shape each into a small, round, flat cake.
3. Heat the oil in a wok (*kadhai*); first dip the potato cakes in the beaten eggs, coat with breadcrumbs, and deep-fry till golden brown. Remove with a slotted spoon and drain the excess oil on absorbent paper towels. Repeat till all the cakes are fried.
4. Serve hot.

Patrel
Colocasia leaf rolls

Preparation time: 30 min.
Cooking time: 30 min.
Serves: **6-8**

Snacks and Starters

Ingredients:

Colocasia leaves (*arvi ka saag*), centre stems removed	30
Gram flour (*besan*)	½ cup / 50 gm
Wholewheat flour (*atta*)	½ cup / 50 gm
Rice flour	½ cup / 60 gm

For the filling:

Dry red chillies (*sookhi lal mirch*)	6
Green chillies	6
Ginger (*adrak*), 1″ piece	1
Garlic (*lasan*)	1 pod
Cumin (*jeera*) seeds, roasted	1 tsp / 2 gm
Coriander (*dhaniya*) seeds, roasted	1 tsp / 2 gm
Cloves (*laung*)	6
Cinnamon (*dalchini*), 1″ stick	1
Turmeric (*haldi*) powder	½ tsp / 1 gm
Bananas, mashed	2
Green coriander (*hara dhaniya*), chopped	2 tbsp / 8 gm
Tamarind (*imli*) water	1 cup / 180 ml
Jaggery (*gur*)	2 tbsp / 40 gm
Salt to taste	
Vegetable oil	6 tbsp / 90 ml

Method:

1. **For the filling**, grind all the ingredients together to make a thick paste, adding a little water if required.

2. Place an inverted colocasia leaf flat, spread the paste thinly over it, place another leaf on top and

apply the paste again. Continue this process for 4-5 leaves if they are large or 8-10 leaves if they are small. Tuck in the sides and roll tightly, secure with a string. Similarly, make more such rolls.

3. Heat the oil in a pan; fry the rolls on all sides, then cover the pan with a lid containing some water.

4. Lower heat, stirring occasionally, for 45 minutes to 1 hour. Remove and keep aside to cool.

5. This can be refrigerated for a week or so and eaten when desired.

6. To serve, cut the rolls into slices and shallow fry.

7. Serve with lemon wedges.

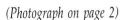

Store Fresh

Store dried fruits, flour, and breadcrumbs in the refrigerator. They will not become rancid or stale.

(Photograph on page 2)

Kervai
Shallow fried banana cakes

Preparation time: 15 min.
Cooking time: 20 min.
Serves: 6

Ingredients:

Bananas, raw, long	6
Ghee	½ tsp / 2 gm
Almonds (*badam*), sliced	½ cup / 60 gm
Raisins (*kishmish*)	½ cup / 50 gm
Cinnamon (*dalchini*) powder	a pinch
Vegetable oil for shallow frying	

Method:

1. Boil the bananas whole, with the skin. To check if done, pierce with a knife, if it goes though remove from heat and keep aside to cool.
2. Then peel and wash. Refrigerate until required.
3. Heat the ghee in a pan; add the almonds, raisins, and cinnamon powder. Sauté till golden, remove and keep aside to cool.
4. Mash a banana, and shape into a round cake. Make a hollow in the centre and stuff with some dried fruit mixture. Seal the filling inside and pat into shape. Repeat till all the cakes are done.
5. Heat the oil in non-stick pan; shallow fry the cakes, on medium heat, till golden. Remove and drain the excess oil on absorbent paper towels.

Tamata Pereeda

Eggs on tomato

Preparation time: 15 min.
Cooking time: 30 min.
Serves: 6-8

Ingredients:

Eggs, separated	4
Tomatoes, ripe, skinned, finely chopped	1 kg
Vegetable oil	3 tbsp / 45 ml
Onions, medium, finely sliced	2
Grind to a paste:	
Cumin (*jeera*) seeds	½ tsp / 1 gm
Garlic (*lasan*), cloves	8
Ginger (*adrak*), 1″ piece	1
Green chillies	4
Dry red chillies (*sookhi lal mirch*)	9
Salt	1 tsp / 4 gm
Jaggery (*gur*)	4 tbsp / 80 gm

Method:

1. Heat the oil in a wok (*kadhai*); add the onions and sauté till light brown. Add the ground paste and salt; sauté for a while.

2. Add the tomatoes and mix well. Add the jaggery and cook on low heat till the mixture is dry. Remove and transfer the contents into an ovenproof dish.

3. Beat the egg whites till frothy. Add the yolks and beat again. Pour this over the tomato mixture and bake in a preheated oven (200°C / 400°F) till the eggs are firm to the touch.

4. Remove and serve with bread.

Kheema Na Pattice
Minced lamb patties

Preparation time: 30 min.
Cooking time: 40 min.
Serves: 6-8

Ingredients:

Lamb mince (*keema*)	750 gm
For the filling:	
Vegetable oil	2 tbsp / 30 ml
Onions	2
Ginger (*adrak*), 1" piece	1
Garlic (*lasan*), cloves	6
Green chillies, seeded	2
Green coriander (*hara dhaniya*)	½ cup / 12 gm
Turmeric (*haldi*) powder	1 tsp / 2 gm
Cumin (*jeera*) powder	2 tsp / 3 gm
Salt to taste	
Lemon (*nimbu*) juice	1 tbsp / 15 ml
Potatoes, boiled, mashed	1½ kg
Refined flour (*maida*)	5 tbsp / 50 gm
Salt to taste	
Vegetable oil for shallow frying	1 cup / 200 ml
Eggs, beaten	4
Breadcrumbs as required	

Method:

1. **For the filling,** heat the oil in a pan; sauté the onions till brown. Add the remaining ingredients (except lemon juice) and the lamb; sauté. Add a little water if required and cook till the lamb is brown and the mixture is completely dry.
2. Now, add the lemon juice. Mix well and keep aside to cool.
3. **For the covering,** mix the mashed potatoes with the refined flour and salt; knead well.

4. Take a spoonful of the potato mixture and flatten it with wet palms. Make a hollow in the centre and stuff 1½ tsp filling. Fold over the edges to seal the filling inside, and shape into a small round or oval cake. Repeat till all the cakes are done.

5. Heat the oil in a frying pan; dip each cake in the egg, coat with breadcrumbs and shallow fry, turning over just once. Remove with a slotted spoon and drain the excess oil on absorbent paper towels. Repeat with the other cakes.

6. Serve hot.

Know Your Eggs

Fresh eggs are rough and chalky
in appearance while the old eggs
are smooth and shiny.

Colmi Na Kabab

Prawn kebab

Preparation time: 45 min.
Cooking time: 15 min.
Serves: 4-6

Ingredients:

Prawns, shelled, deveined	300 gm
Salt to taste	
Worcestershire sauce	½ tbsp / 7½ ml
Green chilli, chopped	1
Onion, large, chopped	1
Garlic (*lasan*), finely chopped	6 pods
Turmeric (*haldi*) powder	1 tsp / 2 gm
Cumin (*jeera*) seeds	1 tsp / 2 gm
Green coriander (*hara dhaniya*), chopped	4 tbsp / 16 gm
Salt and black pepper to taste	
Egg	1
Vegetable oil for deep-frying	

Method:

1. Wash and marinate the prawns with salt. Keep aside for 45 minutes.
2. Wash the prawns again and pound them.
3. Add the rest of the ingredients (except the egg and oil) and pound again until well blended.
4. Now add the egg and mix well. Divide the mixture equally into small balls.
5. Heat the oil in a wok (*kadhai*); deep-fry the balls, a few at a time, until golden brown. Remove with a slotted spoon and drain the excess oil on absorbent paper towels.
6. Serve hot.

Dhansak
Lamb cooked with mixed grams and vegetables

Preparation time: 1 hr.
Cooking time: 30 min.
Serves: 6-8

I n g r e d i e n t s :

Lamb / Chicken, cut into small pieces   1 kg
Vegetable oil   3 tbsp / 45 ml
Onions, finely chopped   3
Ginger-garlic (*adrak-lasan*) paste 2 tbsp / 36 gm
Dhansak masala (see p. 8)   2 tbsp / 20 gm
Lentil (*masoor dal*), washed   ¼ cup / 28 gm
Split red gram (*arhar dal*)   1 cup / 150 gm
Green gram (*sabut moong dal*)   ¼ cup / 75 gm
Bengal gram (*chana dal*)   ¼ cup / 40 gm
Red pumpkin (*lal kaddu*), chopped   50 gm
Aubergine (*baingan*), small, chopped   1
Tomatoes, small, chopped   2
Onion, big, chopped   1
Potato, chopped   1
Fenugreek leaves (*methi*), fresh 2 tbsp / 10 gm

or Dry fenugreek leaves (*kasoori methi*)   1 tsp / ½ gm

M e t h o d :

1. Wash and soak the lentil and the red and green grams separately for 1 hour. Drain and keep aside.
2. Heat the oil in a pan; sauté the onions, ginger-garlic paste, and the *dhansak* masala till brown.
3. Pressure cook the lamb / chicken, lentil, grams, vegetables, and onion mixture with adequate water till the meat is done. Keep aside to cool.
4. Remove the meat pieces; mash and strain the remaining mixture. Then cook for 5-7 minutes. Now add the meat and cook till the mixture becomes thick like a broth. Serve hot.

Rus Chawal

Lamb in a tomato gravy

Preparation time: 15 min.
Cooking time: 30 min.
Serves: 5-7

Lamb

Ingredients:

Lamb, cut into pieces	750 gm
Vegetable oil	½ cup / 100 ml
Onions, large, finely sliced lengthwise	3
Ginger-garlic (*adrak-lasan*) paste	2 tsp / 12 gm
Red chilli powder	1½ tsp / 3 gm
Turmeric (*haldi*) powder	¼ tsp / ½ gm
Salt to taste	
Tomatoes, large, finely sliced	4
Potatoes, peeled, cut lengthwise	250 gm
Green coriander (*hara dhaniya*), finely chopped	1 tbsp / 4 gm

Method:

1. Heat the oil in a large pan; add the onions and sauté till brown. Add the ginger-garlic paste, red chilli powder, turmeric powder, and salt; sauté for about 1 minute.
2. Add the tomatoes and let the mixture simmer till it is absolutely dry.
3. Add the lamb and sauté for some time. Gradually, add about 3 cups water and cook till the lamb is almost done. Add the potatoes and cook till tender.
4. Garnish with green coriander and serve hot with steamed rice.

Gosht Na Vindaloo
Lamb vindaloo

Preparation time: 2 hrs.
Cooking time: I hr.
Serves: 6-7

Ingredients:

Lamb, cut into small cubes	500 gm
Grind to a paste with 2 tbsp vinegar:	
Dry red chillies (*sookhi lal mirch*)	8
Garlic (*lasan*), cloves	6
Ginger (*adrak*), 1″ piece	1
Cloves (*laung*)	3
Green cardamoms (*choti elaichi*)	5
Black peppercorns (*sabut kali mirch*)	6
Cinnamon (*dalchini*), ½″ stick	1
Turmeric (*haldi*) powder	½ tsp / 1 gm
Cumin (*jeera*) seeds	½ tsp / 1 gm
Salt to taste	
Vegetable oil	6 tbsp / 90 ml
Potatoes, small, peeled, cut	3
Onions, sliced	2
Tomatoes, small	3
Green peas (*matar*), boiled	250 gm

Method:

1. Marinate the lamb with the ground spice paste and salt. Keep aside for 2 hours.
2. Heat the oil in a wok (*kadhai*); fry the lamb for 10 minutes. Add 5 cups water and bring the mixture to the boil. Stir occasionally. Cook for about 50 minutes or till the lamb is almost done.
3. Now, add the potatoes, onions, and tomatoes. Cook till the lamb and potatoes are cooked. Finally, add the green peas; mix well and serve.

Lamb

Kheema
Minced lamb

Preparation time: 15 min.
Cooking time: 30 min.
Serves: 6-7

Ingredients:

Lamb mince (*keema*), washed	500 gm
Vegetable oil	2 tbsp / 30 ml
Onions, large, chopped	2-3
Garam masala	1½ tsp / 3 gm
Red chilli powder	1 tsp / 2 gm
Ginger-garlic (*adrak-lasan*) paste	½ tbsp / 9 gm
Tomatoes, medium, chopped	2-3
Fenugreek leaves (*methi*), fresh, chopped	1 tbsp / 5 gm
Vinegar (*sirka*)	½ tbsp / 8 ml
Sugar	¼ tsp
Salt to taste	
Green coriander (*hara dhaniya*) and green chilli for garnish	

Method:

1. Hang the mince in a muslin cloth for a while to drain out the excess water.
2. Heat 1 tbsp oil in a wok (*kadhai*); lightly sauté the onions. Add the garam masala and ginger-garlic paste. Sauté for 5 minutes.
3. Now add the tomatoes and simmer till the water is completely absorbed.
4. Add the mince and fenugreek leaves, mix well. Add vinegar and sugar; cook till the mince is done.
5. Serve hot garnished with green coriander and green chillies.

Masala Ni Kaleji

Fried liver

Preparation time: 20 min.
Cooking time: 15 min.
Serves: 6-8

L a m b

Ingredients:

Lamb's liver, cleaned (membranes removed), cut into 1" pieces	1 kg
Salt to taste	
Grind to a paste:	
Ginger (*adrak*), 2" piece	1
Garlic (*lasan*), cloves	8
Dry red chillies (*sookhi lal mirch*)	6
Turmeric (*haldi*) powder	1 tsp / 2 gm
Cumin (*jeera*) seeds	1 tsp / 2 gm
Vegetable oil	3 tbsp / 45 ml

Method:

1. Marinate the liver with the ground paste and salt.
2. Heat the oil in a pan; shallow fry the liver for 2-3 minutes. Do not over fry as the liver will get tough.
3. Serve hot.

Bafat
Lamb cooked in spiced vinegar

Preparation time: 20 min.
Cooking time: 40 min.
Serves: 6-8

Ingredients:

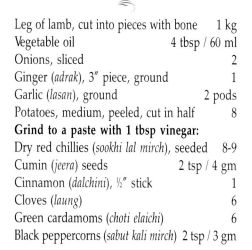

Leg of lamb, cut into pieces with bone	1 kg
Vegetable oil	4 tbsp / 60 ml
Onions, sliced	2
Ginger (*adrak*), 3″ piece, ground	1
Garlic (*lasan*), ground	2 pods
Potatoes, medium, peeled, cut in half	8

Grind to a paste with 1 tbsp vinegar:

Dry red chillies (*sookhi lal mirch*), seeded	8-9
Cumin (*jeera*) seeds	2 tsp / 4 gm
Cinnamon (*dalchini*), ½″ stick	1
Cloves (*laung*)	6
Green cardamoms (*choti elaichi*)	6
Black peppercorns (*sabut kali mirch*)	2 tsp / 3 gm
Tomatoes, chopped	4
Jaggery (*gur*) and salt to taste	

Method:

1. Heat 2 tbsp oil in a pan; add the onions, ginger and garlic; sauté for 2 minutes.
2. Add the lamb and sauté till brown. Add about 1 cup water, lower heat, and simmer till the lamb is almost done. Add the potatoes; mix well.
3. Meanwhile, heat the remaining oil in another pan; sauté the ground paste. Add the tomatoes and cook on low heat for 2 minutes. Transfer the tomato mixture to the lamb mixture. Add jaggery and salt and mix well. Simmer for 10 minutes.
4. Serve hot with chapattis.

Lamb

Dahi Ma Gosht

Lamb cooked in yoghurt and raisins

Preparation time: 20 min.
Cooking time: 40 min.
Serves: 6-7

Ingredients:

Lamb, cut into pieces	1 kg
Vegetable oil	½ cup / 100 ml
Onions, large, finely chopped lengthwise	4
Ginger-garlic (*adrak-lasan*) paste	3 tsp / 18 gm
Dry red chillies (*sookhi lal mirch*)	2 tsp / 4 gm
Yoghurt (*dahi*)	4 cups / 750 gm
Raisins (*kishmish*), finely ground	2 cups / 200 gm
Salt to taste	

Method:

1. Heat the oil in a pressure cooker; sauté the onions till golden brown. Add the ginger-garlic paste and dry red chillies; cook adding 1 tsp yoghurt, at a time, till half the yoghurt is used up. Now add the lamb and mix well.
2. Beat the remaining yoghurt till smooth and add to the lamb mixture. Pressure cook till 3 whistles or till the lamb is tender.
3. If the gravy is too thin, remove the lamb and boil till thick. Return the lamb to the cooker, and mix in the raisins. The gravy should be minimal.
4. Serve hot with chapattis.

Variation: *Chicken can also be used as an alternative.*

Matar Ma Gosht
Lamb cooked with green peas

Preparation time: 15 min.
Cooking time: 30 min.
Serves: 4-6

Ingredients:

Lamb, cut into cubes	350 gm
Green peas (*matar*), shelled	350 gm
Vegetable oil	2 tbsp / 30 ml
Onions, medium, finely sliced	2

Grind to a paste:

Garlic (*lasan*), cloves	6
Ginger (*adrak*), 2 cm piece	1
Turmeric (*haldi*) powder	1 tsp / 2 gm
Parsi *sambhar* masala (see p. 9)	1 tsp / 2 gm
Green coriander (*hara dhaniya*), finely chopped	3 tbsp / 12 gm
Onions, medium, finely chopped	2
Salt to taste	

Method:

1. Heat the oil in a pan; sauté the onions till golden. Remove and drain the excess oil on absorbent paper towels.
2. In the same oil, add the garlic-ginger paste, turmeric powder, and Parsi *sambhar* masala. Cook for 1 minute adding 1 tbsp water, if the paste sticks to the bottom of the pan.
3. Add the lamb and cook on high heat for 3 minutes.
4. Add green peas, green coriander, fried onions, and salt. Mix well. Add 4 cups water, bring to the boil. Lower heat and simmer (covered) till the lamb is tender and about ¾ cup gravy remains.
5. Serve hot.

L a m b

Bhaji Ma Bheja
Brain with spinach

Preparation time: 30 min.
Cooking time: 40 min.
Serves: 6-8

L a m b

Ingredients:

Spinach (*palak*), remove leaves and tender
  stalks, washed, chopped   1 kg
Sheep's brain, soaked in water
  for 30 minutes, drained   3
Vegetable oil   3 tbsp / 45 ml
Onions, medium, finely sliced   2
Grind to a paste:
Garlic (*lasan*), cloves   6
Ginger (*adrak*), 2 cm piece   1
Green chillies   2

Turmeric (*haldi*) powder   1 tsp / 2 gm
Red chilli powder   1½ tsp / 3 gm
Tomatoes, medium, finely chopped   2
Green coriander (*hara dhaniya*),
  finely chopped   3 tbsp / 12 gm
Salt to taste
Vinegar (*sirka*)   3 tsp / 15 ml

Method:

1. Carefully discard the outer skin, blood vessels, and 2 white beads at the base of each brain. Cut the brain into 3-4 pieces.

2. Heat the oil in a pan; sauté the onions till golden brown. Add the green-chilli paste, and the remaining ingredients except the last two; sauté for 2 minutes. Add the spinach and salt; cook covered for 15-20 minutes on medium heat.

3. Mix in the vinegar, stir for 1 minute. Add the brains and cook till tender. Serve hot.

Jardaloo Ma Gosht
Lamb with dried apricots

Preparation time: 4 hrs.
Cooking time: 30 min.
Serves: 4-6

Ingredients:

Lamb, cut	500 gm
Dried apricots (*khumani*), deseeded, soaked for 4 hours	240 gm
Vegetable oil	2 tbsp / 30 ml
Onions, chopped	2-3
Grind to a paste	
Garlic (*lasan*), cloves	6-8
Ginger (*adrak*), 2″ piece	1
Salt to taste	
Cinnamon (*dalchini*), 2″ stick	1
Sugar to taste	

Method:

1. Heat the oil in a wok (*kadhai*); sauté the onions till golden brown. Add the ginger-garlic paste and sauté for 5-8 minutes.
2. Add the lamb, salt, and cinnamon stick. Sauté for a few minutes. Add enough water to cook the lamb till tender.
3. In another pan, brown the sugar. Add the apricots with the soaked water. Bring the mixture to the boil. Lower heat and cook till the apricots turn soft.
4. Mix the apricot mixture with the cooked lamb. Heat again and serve hot.

Kala Masoor Dal Ma Gosht
Lamb in a thick lentil gravy

Preparation time: I hr.
Cooking time: 30-40 min.
Serves: 6-8

Lamb

Ingredients:

Lentil (*masoor dal*), washed, soaked for 1 hour	250 gm
Lamb, cut into pieces	750 gm
Vegetable oil	2 tbsp / 30 ml
Onions, large, chopped lengthwise	3-4
Ginger-garlic (*adrak-lasan*) paste	2 tbsp / 36 gm
Garam masala	1½ tsp / 3 gm
Parsi *sambhar* masala (see p. 9)	1 tsp / 2 gm
Green chillies, whole	4
Turmeric (*haldi*) powder	½ tsp / 1 gm
Salt to taste	
Tomatoes, finely chopped	3-4

Method:

1. Heat the oil in a large pan; sauté the onions till golden brown. Add the ginger-garlic paste, garam masala, Parsi *sambhar* masala, green chillies, turmeric powder, and salt. Sauté for 5-10 minutes.
2. Add the tomatoes and cook on low heat till the water is completely absorbed.
3. Add the lamb and the drained lentil; pressure cook till 3 whistles or till done.
4. Take out a bowlful of lentil from the cooker, mash well and put it back in the cooker. (This is done for a smooth gravy.)
5. Serve hot.

Variation: *This dish can also be made without lamb.*

Parsi Gosht Ne Curry

Lamb curry flavoured with coconut

Preparation time: 30 min.
Cooking time: 40-50 min.
Serves: 4-6

Ingredients:

Lamb, cut into 1″ cubes	500 gm
Vegetable oil	4 tbsp / 60 ml
Onions, large, sliced	4
Ginger (*adrak*), 1″ piece, paste	1
Garlic (*lasan*) pods, paste	10

Roast and grind to a paste:

Coriander (*dhaniya*) seeds	1 tsp / 2 gm
Cumin (*jeera*) seeds	½ tsp / 1 gm
Poppy (*khuskhus*) seeds	3 tsp / 6 gm
Peanuts (*moongphalli*)	2 tsp

Coconut (*nariyal*), grated, ground	½
Tomatoes, large, chopped, peeled	2
Salt to taste	
Dry red chillies (*sookhi lal mirch*)	7
Curry leaves (*kadhi patta*)	4-5

Method:

1. Heat the oil in a pan; sauté the onions until golden brown. Add the ginger-garlic paste and sauté on a low flame for 2 minutes.

2. Add the spice paste; sauté for 2 minutes. Add the coconut and cook till a pleasant aroma emanates. Add the lamb, and the remaining ingredients; sauté for 10 minutes. Gradually, pour in 4 cups water, stirring to blend well. Bring to the boil.

3. Cover the pan, with water on the lid and simmer, stirring occasionally, till the gravy is thick and the lamb is tender. Serve hot with steamed rice.

Lamb

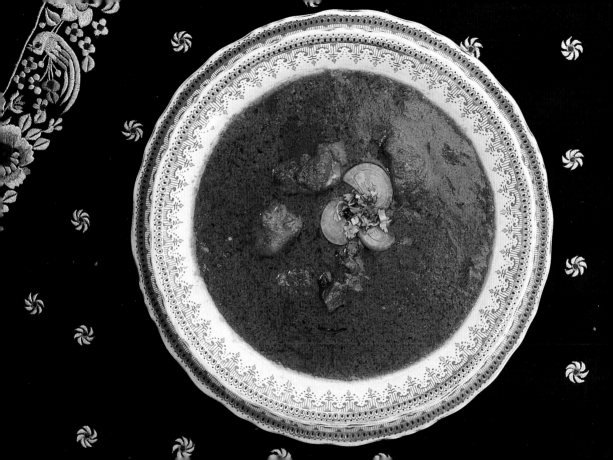

Machhi Patia

Fish in a tomato gravy

Preparation time: 30 min.
Cooking time: 30 min.
Serves: 4-6

Fish and Seafood

Ingredients:

Fish, fillets	750 gm
Salt to taste	
Lemon (*nimbu*) juice	1
Sesame (*til*) seed oil	4 tbsp / 60 ml
Onions, medium, grated	8

Grind with a little vinegar:

Garlic (*lasan*), cloves	6-8
Dry red chillies (*sookhi lal mirch*)	6-8
Cumin (*jeera*) seeds	2 tsp / 4 gm
Vinegar (*sirka*)	1 tbsp / 15 ml
Salt to taste	
Sugar to taste	
Tomatoes, ripe, made into a thick purée	3

Method:

1. Marinate the fish with salt and lemon juice; keep aside for 30 minutes.
2. Heat the sesame seed oil in a pan; sauté the onions till brown. Add the ground paste and mix well. Add the fish and simmer till tender.
3. Add the vinegar, salt, sugar, and tomato purée. Mix well.
4. Serve hot with steamed rice.

Patra Ne Machhi

Chutney fish steamed in banana leaves

Preparation time: 40 min.
Cooking time: 30 min.
Serves: 6-8

Ingredients:

Pomfrets, deboned, cut into ½"-thick slices, washed	2 kg / 2 large
Salt to taste	
Lemon (*nimbu*) juice	1
Coconut (*nariyal*), fresh, grated	1
Green chillies, seeded	3
Green coriander (*hara dhaniya*)	2 cups / 50 gm
Ginger (*adrak*)	1 tbsp / 24 gm
Garlic (*lasan*)	1 pod
Banana leaves or aluminium foil paper	4-5

Method:

1. Marinate the fish with salt and half the lemon juice for 30 minutes to 1 hour.

2. Grind the coconut, green chillies, green coriander, ginger, and garlic to a smooth paste. Add salt and the remaining lemon juice.

3. Wash the marinated fish and apply the coconut paste on both sides of the fish.

4. Cut the banana leaves large enough to wrap each piece of fish. Spread a little oil over the leaves and wrap each piece like a parcel. Tie with a cotton thread, and steam in a large steamer for 20 minutes. It can also be baked in an oven at 180°C / 360°F for 15 minutes.

5. Remove the string and serve.

Sas Ni Machhi

Sweet and sour fish

Preparation time: 20 min.
Cooking time: 20 min.
Serves: 6-8

Ingredients:

Pomfret, fillets or cut into ½"-thick slices   1 kg
Vegetable oil   2 tbsp / 30 ml
Onion, large, finely chopped   1
Rice flour   1 tbsp / 10 gm
Cumin (*jeera*), coarsely powdered   1 tsp / 2 gm
Garlic (*lasan*), pods, finely chopped   2
Green chillies, seeded, chopped   8
Water   3 cups / 600 ml
Salt to taste
Eggs, beaten   3
Sugar   1 tsp / 3 gm
Vinegar (*sirka*)   ½ cup / 100 ml
Green coriander (*hara dhaniya*),
   chopped   3 tbsp / 12 gm

Method:

1. Heat the oil in a broad pan; sauté the onion till light brown. Add the rice flour, sauté for 2 minutes. Add the cumin powder, garlic, and green chillies; sauté for 1 minute. Add water and salt.

2. Bring the mixture to the boil. Add the fish and simmer till it is almost done. Remove from heat.

3. Mix the sugar and vinegar with the beaten eggs.

4. Pour the egg mixture into the pan and swirl it around, taking care not to break the fish.

5. Return the pan to the heat and simmer till the gravy thickens. Adjust the vinegar and sugar to get a sweet and sour taste.

6. Serve hot garnished with green coriander.

Tareli Machhi
Fried fish

Preparation time: 30 min.
Cooking time: 20 min.
Serves: 6-8

Ingredients:

Fish, fillets or cut into ½"-thick
    slices   6 large or 12 small
For the marinade:
Turmeric (*haldi*) powder   1 tsp / 2 gm
Red chilli powder   1 tsp / 2 gm
Cumin (*jeera*) powder (optional) 1 tsp / 1½ gm
Lemon (*nimbu*) juice   1
Salt to taste

Sesame (*til*) seed oil   1 cup / 200 ml

Method:

1. Mix all the ingredients for the marinade and rub into the fish. Marinate for about 30 minutes.
2. Heat the oil in a frying pan; fry the fish on low heat till crisp. Remove with a slotted spoon and drain the excess oil on absorbent paper towels.
3. Serve immediately with lemon slices.

Parsi Colmi Papeta
Parsi prawn with potatoes

Preparation time: I hr.
Cooking time: 40 min.
Serves: 4-6

Fish and Seafood

Ingredients:

Prawns, raw, shelled, deveined,
   washed — 450 gm
Lemon (*nimbu*) juice — 2 tsp / 10 ml
Salt to taste
Grind to a paste:
Dry red chillies (*sookhi lal mirch*),
   soaked in 1½ tbsp malt vinegar — 6
Cumin (*jeera*) seeds — 1 tsp / 2 gm
Garlic (*lasan*), cloves — 4-5
Turmeric (*haldi*) powder — ½ tsp / 1 gm
Onion, small, chopped — 1

Potatoes, peeled, cut into 1 cm cubes — 450 gm
Vegetable oil — 2 tbsp / 30 ml
Curry leaves (*kadhi patta*) — 5-6

Green garlic, cloves and shoots, fresh, chopped — 8
Green chillies, finely chopped — 2
Salt to taste
Green coriander (*hara dhaniya*),
   fresh, finely chopped — 2 tbsp / 8 gm
Eggs (optional) — 2

Method:

1. Marinate the prawns with the lemon juice and some salt. Keep aside.
2. Grind all the ingredients mentioned to a smooth paste, adding a little vinegar if necessary.
3. Mix this paste with the potatoes and keep aside to marinate for at least 1 hour.
4. Heat the oil in a large pan over medium heat; sauté

the curry leaves, green garlic, and green chillies for 2-3 minutes. Add the marinated potatoes.

5. Sauté for 5 minutes, stirring frequently, with a wooden spoon, scraping the base of the pan. Add just enough water to cover the potatoes.

6. Lower heat and simmer, covered, for about 40 minutes or until the potatoes are almost done. The sauce should be thick and rich, if it is too watery, simmer for a while longer. Increase heat and add the prawns. Cook for 2-3 minutes until done.

7. Season with salt and garnish with green coriander.

8. If you are using the eggs, fry them first and then serve on top of the potatoes. This goes well with chapattis.

⟿

Free Flowing
Add a pinch of arrowroot in
salt to avoid lumping.

⟿

Sali Ma Murgh
Chicken with potato straws

Preparation time: 30 min.
Cooking time: 40 min.
Serves: 6-7

Chicken

Ingredients:

Chicken, cut into 8 pieces	1 kg
Vegetable oil	2 tbsp / 30 ml
Cumin (*jeera*) seeds	½ tsp / 1 gm
Curry leaves (*kadhi patta*)	4-5
Onions, large, chopped	2

Grind to a paste:

Garlic (*lasan*), cloves	6
Ginger (*adrak*), ½" piece	1
Cinnamon (*dalchini*), 1" stick	1
Garam masala	1 tsp / 2 gm
Turmeric (*haldi*) powder	½ tsp / 1 gm

Salt to taste

Green chillies	4
Sali (potato straws), available in convenience store	500 gm

Method:

1. Heat the oil in a wok (*kadhai*); add the cumin seeds and curry leaves. When they start spluttering, add the onions and sauté until golden.
2. Add the ground paste and sauté for a minute.
3. Now, add the chicken and salt; keep stirring until the mixture is completely dry.
4. Add 3 cups water and bring the mixture to the boil. Then simmer, stirring occasionally, until the gravy turns thick and the chicken is tender.
5. Transfer the chicken into a dish and sprinkle the *sali* over it.

Aleti Paleti
Spicy chicken liver

Preparation time: 15 min.
Cooking time: 20 min.
Serves: 6-7

Ingredients:

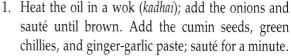

Chicken liver and gizzard, cleaned, cut into ½" pieces	500 gm
Vegetable oil as required	
Onions, chopped	2
Cumin (*jeera*) seeds	1 tsp / 2 gm
Green chillies, slit	2
Ginger-garlic (*adrak-lasan*) paste	1 tsp / 6 gm
Salt to taste	
Tomatoes, chopped	1 tbsp
Jaggery (*gur*), chopped	1 tbsp / 20 gm
Green coriander (*hara dhaniya*), chopped	1 tbsp / 4 gm

Method:

1. Heat the oil in a wok (*kadhai*); add the onions and sauté until brown. Add the cumin seeds, green chillies, and ginger-garlic paste; sauté for a minute.
2. Add the liver, gizzard, and salt; sauté until the liver is cooked. Remove only the liver from the wok and keep aside.
3. Cook the gizzard a little more with water and then add the liver again.
4. Add the tomatoes and jaggery; cook until the mixture is absolutely dry.
5. Serve hot garnished with green coriander.

Lagan Na Chicken Farcha
Chicken deep-fried with egg

Preparation time: 4 hrs.
Cooking time: 30 min.
Serves: 6

Ingredients:

Chicken, with skin, cut into 4-5 pieces   1 kg
Salt to taste
Grind to a paste with 4 tsp vinegr:
Garlic (*lasan*), cloves   6-8
Cumin (*jeera*) seeds   1¼ tsp / 2½ gm
Dry red chillies (*sookhi lal mirch*)   8-10

Breadcrumbs   ½ cup / 60 gm
Eggs   2
Vegetable oil for deep-frying

Method:

1. Boil the chicken with water to cover. Add 1¼ tsp salt; simmer till tender. Keep aside to cool. Prick the pieces with a fork.
2. Add a little salt to the chilli paste, rub over the chicken and keep aside for 4 hours.
3. Coat each piece, on all sides, with breadcrumbs.
4. Heat the oil in a frying pan. Beat the eggs with 1 tsp water till frothy. Dip the chicken into the egg and slide it in the hot oil. Immediately trickle 1 tsp egg over the chicken, simultaneously spooning the hot oil over the egg as it falls on the chicken.
5. Add 4 tsp of beaten egg in the same way. When the egg is golden brown and frilly, remove and keep aside. (Do not turn the chicken over while cooking.) Repeat till all are done. Serve hot.

Badami Murgh
Chicken flavoured with almonds

Preparation time: 4 hrs.
Cooking time: 30 min.
Serves: 6-8

Ingredients:

Chicken, cut into pieces	1½ kg

For the marinade:

Almond (*badam*) paste (powdered almonds can also be used if available)	5 tbsp / 75 gm
Yoghurt (*dahi*), hung for 2 hours	1 cup / 180 gm
Ginger (*adrak*) paste	4 tsp / 24 gm
Garlic (*lasan*) paste	4 tsp / 24 gm
Salt to taste	
Black pepper (*kali mirch*) powder	1 tsp / 2 gm
Lemon (*nimbu*) juice	2 tbsp / 30 ml
Green chillies, chopped	4
Vegetable oil	2 tbsp / 30 ml
Onions, finely sliced	1 cup / 240 gm
Cumin (*jeera*) seeds	1 tsp / 2 gm
Capsicum (*Shimla mirch*), optional	100 gm
Butter, preferably white	4 tbsp / 80 gm
Saffron (*kesar*), dissolved in water	a few strands
Green coriander (*hara dhaniya*), finely chopped	1 tbsp / 4 gm
Green chillies, finely chopped	2

Method:

1. Mix all the ingredients for the marinade. Rub the paste over the chicken and marinate for 4 hours.
2. Heat the oil in a pan; add the onions and cumin seeds; sauté till light brown. Add the chicken without the marinade and sauté till pale brown.
3. Now add the rest of the marinade. When the chicken is half done, add the capsicum (optional)

and the butter. When the chicken is nearly done, add the saffron water and cook, covered, till done.

4. Serve hot garnished with green coriander and green chillies.

Sun the Onions

If you leave chopped onions in bright sunlight for a few hours, it will consume less oil and turn golden immediately.

Lagan Na Tarkari Per Eda
Egg yolks on spicy tomato mixture

Preparation time: 20 min.
Cooking time: 20 min.
Serves: 6-8

Ingredients:

Eggs	8
Vegetable oil	5 tbsp / 75 ml
Ginger-garlic (*adrak-lasan*) paste	1 tsp / 6 gm
Green chillies, deseeded, finely chopped	4
Tomatoes, large, skinned, deseeded	3
Green coriander (*hara dhaniya*), cleaned, washed, finely chopped	½ cup / 12 gm
Vinegar (*sirka*)	1 tbsp / 15 ml
Red chilli powder	½ tsp / 1 gm
Garam masala	½ tsp / 1 gm
Salt to taste	
Onions, sliced, deep-fried	3

Method:

1. Heat the oil in a large heavy-bottomed pan; add the ginger-garlic paste and sauté over medium heat for 2 minutes.

2. Add the green chillies, tomatoes, green coriander, vinegar, red chilli powder, and garam masala. Cook till the tomatoes turn soft. Mix in the salt and the fried onions.

3. Flatten the mixture evenly and make 8 depressions in the mixture. Lower heat.

4. Break each egg separately in a saucer and slip it in a depression. Repeat till all the depressions are covered with egg yolks. Sprinkle lightly with salt.

5. Cook covered till the yolks are done. Do not allow the eggs to become hard. Serve immediately.

Egg

Akoori
Spicy scrambled eggs

Preparation time: 15 min.
Cooking time: 20 min.
Serves: 7-8

Egg

Ingredients:

Eggs	6
Ghee	3 tbsp / 45 gm
Onions, large, chopped	2
Cumin (*jeera*) seeds	½ tsp / 1 gm
Green chillies, finely chopped	3
Garlic (*lasan*), cloves, chopped	2
Turmeric (*haldi*) powder	½ tsp / 1 gm
Salt to taste	
Tomato, large, chopped	1
Green coriander (*hara dhaniya*), chopped	2 tbsp / 8 gm

Method:

1. Heat the ghee in a wok (*kadhai*); add the onions and sauté until golden brown. Add the cumin seeds, green chillies, garlic, turmeric powder, and salt; sauté for 1-2 minutes.
2. Add the tomato and sauté for another minute.
3. Lightly beat the eggs and add to the above mixture. Mix thoroughly and cook for 2-3 minutes.
4. Garnish with green coriander and serve immediately on toast.

Khatu Meethu Stew

Sweet and sour vegetable stew

Preparation time: 30 min.
Cooking time: 30 min.
Serves: 8

Ingredients:

Green peas (*matar*), shelled	250 gm
French beans, trimmed, cubed	150 gm
Carrots (*gajar*), peeled, cut into pieces	4
Cauliflower (*phool gobi*)	300 gm
Baby potatoes, peeled	300 gm
or Potatoes, large, peeled, cut into cubes	3
Yam (*jimikand*), peeled, cut into cubes	300 gm
Sweet potatoes (*shakarkand*), medium, peeled, cut into pieces	2
Baby onions, peeled	300 gm
Vegetable oil	½ cup / 100 ml
Onions, sliced	3
Tomatoes, finely chopped	3
Green chillies, finely chopped	3-4
Green coriander (*hara dhaniya*), finely chopped	3 tbsp / 12 gm
Mint (*pudina*) leaves, finely chopped	¾ cup / 12 gm
Garlic (*lasan*), finely chopped	1 pod
Vinegar (*sirka*)	3 tbsp / 45 ml
Sugar	2 tbsp / 40 gm
Salt to taste	

Method:

1. Heat the oil in a pan; shallow fry the first 8 vegetables, separately.
2. Heat 2 tbsp oil in a pan; sauté the onions till light brown. Add the remaining vegetables; simmer for 3-4 minutes. Mix in the fried vegetables.
3. Add the remaining ingredients; simmer for 5 more minutes. This a sweet and sour preparation.

Lagansala Stew
Wedding stew

Preparation time: 30 min.
Cooking time: 20 min.
Serves: 6-8

I n g r e d i e n t s :

Yam (*jimikand*), cut into small cubes	50 gm
Sweet potatoes (*shakarkand*), cubed	2
French beans, cubed	50 gm
Capsicum (*Shimla mirch*), cubed	1
Carrots (*gajar*), cubed	4
Green peas (*matar*), shelled, boiled	200 gm
Celery, finely chopped, boiled	20 gm
Vegetable oil	1 cup / 200 ml
Onions, large, chopped	2
Green chillies, chopped	3
Cumin-coriander (*jeera-dhaniya*) powder	1 tsp / 2 gm
Turmeric (*haldi*) powder	½ tsp / 1 gm
Ginger-garlic (*adrak-lasan*) paste	1 tsp / 6 gm
Tomatoes, chopped	2
Salt to taste	
Vinegar (*sirka*)	1 tbsp / 15 ml
Worcestershire sauce	1 tbsp / 15 ml

M e t h o d :

1. Heat the oil in a wok (*kadhai*); fry all the cubed vegetables, separately. Keep aside.
2. In the same oil, sauté the onions until soft. Add green chillies, spices, and garlic-ginger paste; sauté for 2 minutes. Add the fried and boiled vegetables, tomatoes, and salt. Cook covered with a heavy lid, containing a little water, until the mixture is reasonably dry. Stir occasionally.
3. Add vinegar and Worcestershire sauce, mix well.
4. Serve hot garnished with green coriander.

Vegetarian

Khara Papeta
A simple potato preparation

Preparation time: 15 min.
Cooking time: 30 min.
Serves: 4-6

Ingredients:

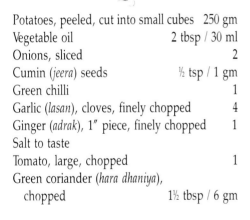

Potatoes, peeled, cut into small cubes	250 gm
Vegetable oil	2 tbsp / 30 ml
Onions, sliced	2
Cumin (*jeera*) seeds	½ tsp / 1 gm
Green chilli	1
Garlic (*lasan*), cloves, finely chopped	4
Ginger (*adrak*), 1" piece, finely chopped	1
Salt to taste	
Tomato, large, chopped	1
Green coriander (*hara dhaniya*), chopped	1½ tbsp / 6 gm

Method:

1. Heat the oil in a wok (*kadhai*); sauté the onions until golden.
2. Add cumin seeds, green chilli, garlic, and ginger. Sauté for a minute.
3. Add the potatoes and salt; sauté for 2 minutes.
4. Add ½ cup water and cook on a low flame until the potatoes are tender and the mixture is absolutely dry. Add the tomato and cook for 5 minutes more.
5. Serve hot garnished with green coriander.

Dhan Dar

Split red gram tempered with garlic

Preparation time: 30 min.
Cooking time: 20 min.
Serves: 4-6

Ingredients:

Split red gram (*arhar dal*)	½ cup / 80 gm
Salt	¼ tsp / 1 gm
Turmeric (*haldi*) powder	¼ tsp / ½ gm
For the tempering:	
Vegetable oil	2 tbsp / 30 ml
Green chillies	2
Salt	a pinch
Garlic (*lasan*) paste	¼ tsp / 1½ gm
or Garlic (*lasan*), cloves, chopped	4-5
Cumin (*jeera*) seeds or powder	¼ tsp / ½ gm

Method:

1. Soak the split red gram in 2-3 cups water with salt and turmeric powder for at least 20 minutes. Most of the water should be absorbed.

2. Transfer the split red gram into a pressure cooker. Add water, about ½" above the dal level. Cook on high heat. After the first whistle, turn heat to low and cook for 5 minutes. Keep aside to cool.

3. Whisk or blend, adding water, if required. Return the cooker to heat and bring it to the boil.

4. **For the tempering**, heat the oil in a pan till smoking; lower heat, sauté all the ingredients till golden. Remove from heat, pour into the dal, and cover immediately to prevent the aroma from escaping.

5. Simmer for 2-3 minutes before serving, garnished with fried onions and a dollop of butter.

Tamata Ne Papeta Nu Stew

Tomato and potato stew

Preparation time: 10 min.
Cooking time: 30 min.
Serves: 4-6

Vegetarian

Ingredients:

Tomatoes	500 gm
Potatoes, peeled, quartered	250 gm
Vegetable oil	2 tbsp / 30 ml
Onion, large, finely sliced	1
Grind to a paste:	
Garlic (*lasan*), cloves	6
Green chillies	3
Cumin (*jeera*) seeds	1 tsp / 2 gm
Green coriander (*hara dhaniya*), chopped	2 tbsp / 8 gm
Water	¼ cup / 50 ml
Salt to taste	
Jaggery (*gur*) or sugar	2 tbsp / 40 gm

Method:

1. Boil the tomatoes for a minute, drain and keep aside to cool. Then peel and chop.
2. Alternatively, blend the tomatoes for a few seconds without boiling or peeling them.
3. Heat the oil in a pan; add the onion and sauté till golden brown. Remove and drain the excess oil.
4. Add the green chilli paste and sauté for a minute or so. Add the potatoes and water; cook covered, on low heat, for 5 minutes.
5. Add the chopped tomatoes or tomato purée and salt; continue to cook for 10 more minutes.
6. Add the jaggery or sugar and cook covered till the potatoes turn soft.

Vegna Khatta Meetha

Sweet and sour aubergines

Preparation time: 15 min.
Cooking time: 30 min.
Serves: 4-6

Ingredients:

Aubergines (*baingan*), cut into ½″ cubes	750 gm
Vegetable oil	¾ cup / 150 ml
Curry leaves (*kadhi patta*)	10
Green chilli, finely chopped	1

Grind to a paste with 2-3 tbsp vinegar:

Garlic (*lasan*), cloves	10
Cumin (*jeera*) seeds	1½ tsp / 3 gm
Coriander (*dhaniya*) seeds	3 tsp / 6 gm
Dry red chillies (*sookhi lal mirch*)	6

Jaggery (*gur*) or sugar	1½ tbsp / 30 gm
Salt to taste	
Vinegar (*sirka*)	2 tbsp / 30 ml

Method:

1. In a wide-bottomed pan, heat the oil till hot. Add the aubergines and fry for a few minutes till light brown. Remove with a slotted spoon and drain the excess oil on absorbent paper towels. Keep aside.

2. In the same oil (add a little more oil if needed), add the curry leaves, green chilli, and the red chilli paste; sauté for 2 minutes. Add the aubergines and mix well.

3. Add jaggery or sugar, salt, and vinegar; cook covered, on medium heat, till the aubergines turn soft. Serve hot.

Brown Chawal

Brown cinnamon rice

Preparation time: 30 min.
Cooking time: 30 min.
Serves: 6-8

Ingredients:

Rice, Basmati, washed and soaked for 30 minutes	2 cups / 400 gm
Vegetable oil	1 tbsp / 15 ml
Cinnamon (*dalchini*), 1" stick	1
Sugar	2 tbsp / 40 gm
Water	4 cups / 800 ml
Salt	1 tsp / 4 gm
Onions, sliced, fried	2

Method:

1. Heat the oil in a heavy-bottomed pan; add the cinnamon stick and sugar. Stir continuously, on low heat, till the sugar caramalises (ensuring that the sugar does not burn).

2. Add the water and salt. Bring the mixture to the boil. Now add the rice and cook covered, on low heat, for about 20 minutes.

3. Serve hot garnished with fried onions.

Parsi Biryani
Flavoured rice mixed with spicy meat

Preparation time: 20 min.
Cooking time: 50 min.
Serves: 6-8

Ingredients:

Lamb / Chicken, cut into pieces   1 kg
Rice, Basmati or any other
   good quality rice   3¼ cups / 650 gm
Vegetable oil   ½ cup / 100 ml
Onions, large, chopped lengthwise   4
Ginger-garlic (*adrak-lasan*) paste 1 tbsp / 18 gm
Red chilli powder   1 tsp / 2 gm
Black peppercorns
   (*sabut kali mirch*)   ½ tsp / 1 gm
Cloves (*laung*)   ½ tsp / 1 gm
Cinnamon (*dalchini*), 1" sticks   ½ tsp / 1 gm
Green cardamoms (*choti elaichi*)   ½ tsp / 1 gm
Mace (*javitri*)   ½ tsp / 1 gm
Yoghurt (*dahi*), sour   1 cup / 180 gm
Salt to taste

Yellow food colour, dissolved in ¼ cup milk   a few drops
Saffron (*kesar*)   a few strands

Method:

1. Heat the oil in a wok (*kadhai*); fry only half the onions till brown. Remove with a slotted spoon and drain the excess oil on absorbent paper towels. Keep aside.

2. In the same oil, fry the remaining onions till transparent. Add the ginger-garlic paste and sauté. Add the red chilli powder and the whole spices; sauté slightly.

3. Now add the lamb / chicken and cook on medium heat. When the water evaporates, add the yoghurt gradually, bit by bit, till all is used up. Add just

enough water to cook the lamb / chicken till tender. There should be no gravy left.

4. Boil the rice in plenty of water with salt. When almost done drain it.

5. In a large vessel, spread a layer of rice, then a layer of cooked lamb / chicken, and some fried onions. Continue the layering till all the rice and lamb / chicken are used up. Top with fried onions.

6. Mix the saffron with the yellow food colour mixture and pour it over the rice mixture. Do not mix the rice at this point.

7. Bake in the oven for 30 minutes. Remove from the oven and immediately cover the rice with a wet cloth. Then place a lid on the vessel.

8. Before serving, remove the cloth and lid and serve the *biryani* on a big, rice platter.

Worm-Free Rice

To protect rice from worms, put a few garlic flakes in the container.

Machhi Nu Pulao
Fish rice cooked in coconut milk

Preparation time: 30 min.
Cooking time: 30 min.
Serves: 6-8

Ingredients:

Rice, washed,
   soaked for 30 minutes   2 cups / 400 gm
Pomfret, fillet, cut into large pieces   1 large
Salt to taste
Vegetable oil or ghee   5 tbsp / 75 ml
Onions, large, sliced   5
Grind to a paste:
Cumin (*jeera*) seeds, roasted   2 tsp / 4 gm
Cinnamon (*dalchini*), 1" stick   1
Cloves (*laung*)   2
Turmeric (*haldi*) powder   ½ tsp / 1 gm
Green cardamoms (*choti elaichi*)   5
Garlic (*lasan*), cloves   7
Dry red chillies (*sookhi lal mirch*)   7
Coconut (*nariyal*), grated   200 gm

Salt to taste

Coconut (*nariyal*) milk   3 cups / 600 ml
Green coriander (*hara dhaniya*), chopped   1 cup / 25 gm

Method:

1. Marinate the fish with salt for a few minutes.
2. Heat the oil in a wok (*kadhai*); sauté the onions till brown. Add the ground paste; sauté for 2 minutes.
3. Wash the marinated fish and then add to the wok.
4. Add the rice, coconut milk and half of the green coriander. Bring the mixture to the boil. Lower heat and simmer until the rice is cooked. If more water is required, use only hot water. Serve hot, garnished with the remaining green coriander.

Mithu Dhai

Sweet yoghurt

Preparation time: 5 min.
Cooking time: 20 min.
Serves: 6-8

A c c o m p a n i m e n t s

Ingredients:

Milk	2¼ cups / 500 ml
Sugar	4 tsp / 12 gm
Yoghurt (*dahi*)	1 tsp / 10 gm
Nutmeg-green cardamom (*jaiphal-choti elaichi*) powder	1 tsp / 3 gm

Method:

1. Bring the milk to the boil in a pan.
2. Lower heat, add the sugar and simmer, uncovered, for 15-20 minutes.
3. Remove the pan from the heat and keep aside to cool till lukewarm.
4. Smear the bowl with the yoghurt.
5. Pour the milk into the bowl and stir 3 or 4 times.
6. Keep covered for several hours or overnight, till the yoghurt sets. Then keep in the refrigerator.
7. Sprinkle with nutmeg-green cardamom powder before serving.

Ambakalio

Mango cooked in jaggery

Preparation time: 15 min.
Cooking time: 20 min.
Serves: 4-6

Ingredients:

Mango, large, peeled, sliced	1
Ghee or butter	3 tbsp / 45 gm
Onion, large, sliced	1
Cinnamon (*dalchini*), 1" stick	1
Cloves (*laung*)	4-6
Green cardamoms (*choti elaichi*)	4-6
Jaggery (*gur*)	6¼ tsp / 125 gm
Green chillies, seeded, chopped	2
Green coriander (*hara dhaniya*), chopped	1 tbsp / 4 gm
Salt	½ tsp / 2 gm
Water	½ cup / 100 ml

Method:

1. Heat the ghee or butter in a pan; add the onion, cinnamon stick, cloves, and green cardamoms. Sauté till light brown.
2. Add the jaggery, mango, green chillies, green coriander, salt, and water. Simmer for 1-2 minutes and mix gently without breaking the mango slices.
3. Serve with *dhansak* (see p. 20).

Khatte Meethe Mango Chutney

Sweet and sour mango chutney

Preparation time: 15 min.
Cooking time: 25 min.

Accompaniments

Ingredients:

Green mangoes, large, raw, peeled, sliced	2 kg
Sugar	2 kg
Aniseed (*saunf*)	4 tbsp / 20 gm
Salt	2 tbsp / 16 gm
Red chilli powder to taste	
Dry red chillies (*sookhi lal mirch*) according to taste	
Malt vinegar (*sirka*)	1 cup / 200 ml

Method:

1. Mix the sugar and mangoes together thoroughly in a large pan.
2. Add the remaining ingredients (except vinegar) and cook on low heat till the sugar dissolves.
3. When the mangoes are soft, add the malt vinegar. Cook for a few minutes till the syrup is quite thick.
4. Be careful not to over cook as the consistency will become thick when the mixture cools. Store in airtight jars.

Lagan Nu Achar
Wedding pickle

Preparation time: 45 min. - 1 hr.
Cooking time: 30-45 min.

Ingredients:

Dried dates (*khajoor*), finely chopped	100 gm
Raisins (*kishmish*)	3 cups / 300 gm
Dried apricots (*khumani*)	300 gm
Sugar	2 kg
Carrots (*gajar*), grated	2 kg
Jaggery (*gur*)	250 gm
Vinegar (*sirka*)	3¾ cups / 750 ml
Ginger (*adrak*), julienned	50 gm
Garlic (*lasan*), sliced	100 gm
Salt to taste	
Dry red chillies (*sookhi lal mirch*)	15
Garam masala	2 tbsp / 10 gm

Method:

1. Soak the dates, raisins, and apricots overnight in 1 cup sugar and as much vinegar as necessary.

2. In a heavy-bottomed pan, cook the carrots, the remaining sugar, jaggery, and 500 ml of vinegar over low heat. When soft, add ginger, garlic, and salt; cook till the mixture becomes a sticky syrup.

3. Add the dates, raisins and apricot mixture; bring to the boil. Add the dry red chillies and garam masala, remove the pan from the heat. Keep aside to cool and store in airtight jars.

4. This pickle can be preserved for several years if handled properly and kept in a cool, dark place.

Vegna Achar
Aubergine pickle

Preparation time: 20 min.
Cooking time: 20 min.

Ingredients:

Aubergines (*baingan*), washed, dried, cut into ½″ cubes	350 gm
Vegetable oil	1 tbsp / 15 ml

Grind to a fine paste with 1-2 tsp of vinegar:

Garlic (*lasan*), cloves	4
Ginger (*adrak*), 1″ piece	1
Dry red chillies (*sookhi lal mirch*)	5
Turmeric (*haldi*) powder	¼ tsp / ½ gm

Jaggery (*gur*)	2½ tbsp / 50 gm
Vinegar (*sirka*)	½ cup / 100 ml
Salt to taste	

Pound together:

Green cardamoms (*choti elaichi*)	3
Cinnamon (*dalchini*), ¼″ stick	1
Cloves (*laung*)	2
Black peppercorns (*sabut lal mirch*)	4

Method:

1. Heat the oil in a pan; add the ground paste and sauté for 3 minutes. Add the aubergines and cook till almost done.
2. Add the jaggery, vinegar, and salt; mix well. Lower heat and simmer till the oil floats on top.
3. Add the pounded spices, mix well and keep aside to cool.
4. Store in airtight jars.

Colmi Nu Achar

Fresh prawn pickle

Preparation time: 20 min.
Cooking time: 20 min.

Ingredients:

Prawns, fresh, shelled, deveined	3 cups
Turmeric (*haldi*) powder	1 tsp / 2 gm
Mustard oil or vegetable oil	½ cup / 100 ml
Salt to taste	
Onions, large, minced	5

Grind to a paste:

Garlic (*lasan*), cloves	12
Dry red chillies (*sookhi lal mirch*)	12
Curry leaves (*kadhi patta*)	a few
Vinegar (*sirka*)	½ cup / 100 ml

Method:

1. Remove the heads from the prawns and wash well in salt water. Drain till absolutely dry. Mix with turmeric powder and keep aside for 10 minutes.
2. Heat the oil in a pan; fry the prawns with some salt till crisp. Remove and keep aside.
3. Reheat the oil till smoking; sauté the onions until golden brown. Add the ground paste and sauté for a few minutes. Add the curry leaves and vinegar.
4. When the mixture starts to boil, add the prawns and salt to taste. Lower heat and simmer until the mixture is dry. Remove the pan from the heat and keep aside to cool completely.
5. Store in a glass jar and refrigerate until required.

Bhakra
Deep-fried flour puffs

Preparation time: 25 min.+ overnight
Cooking time: 30 min.
Makes: 20 pcs.

Ingredients:

Sugar	1 kg
Eggs	6
Semolina (*suji*), sifted	1 kg
Refined flour (*maida*), sifted	1 kg
Toddy	1 lt
Ghee	1¼ cups / 240 gm
Nutmeg (*jaiphal*) powder	1 tsp / 2 gm
Green cardamoms (*choti elaichi*), peeled, powdered	6
Onion seeds (*kalonji*), crushed	50 gm
Vanilla essence	1 tsp / 5 ml
Baking powder	2 tsp / 8 gm
Refined flour (*maida*)	2½ cups / 250 gm
Vegetable oil for deep-frying	2 cups / 400 ml

Method:

1. Mix the sugar and eggs in a large bowl until the sugar dissolves. Add the next 8 ingredients and knead well.

2. Add the baking powder and knead once again to make a thick dough (if required, sprinkle a little cold water). Cover with a lid and keep a heavy weight over it. Let the dough stand overnight or for about 12 hours.

3. Next day, sprinkle a little flour on the dough and divide it into 4-5 portions. Roll each out into a large round about a ¼" thick. With a round biscuit cutter, 1½" in diameter, cut out discs.

4. Deep-fry the discs in hot oil until dark brown. Remove and repeat till all are fried. Serve with tea.

Dar Ni Pori

Stuffed red gram wheat and rice cake

Preparation time: I hr.
Cooking time: 25-30 min.
Makes: 2

Ingredients:

For the rice crust:

Rice flour	10 tbsp / 100 gm
Ghee	½ cup / 90 gm
Salt	a pinch

For the wheat flour rounds:

Semolina (*suji*)	1 cup / 100 gm
Wholewheat flour (*atta*)	5 tbsp / 50 gm
Salt	a pinch
Water	½ cup / 100 ml
Rose water (*gulab jal*)	1 tsp / 5 ml
Ghee	1 tsp / 4 gm

For the stuffing:

Split red gram (*arhar dal*), washed, drained	1½ cups / 240 gm
Sugar	275 gm
Nutmeg-cardamom (*jaiphal-elaichi*) powder	2 tsp / 4 gm
Vanilla essence	1 tsp / 5 ml
Ghee	6 tbsp / 90 gm
Black cumin (*shah jeera*) seeds, grounded	½ tsp / 1 gm
Raisins (*kishmish*)	1 tbsp / 10 gm
Crystallised cherries, finely chopped	15 gm
Onion seeds (*kalonji*)	10 gm

Method:

1. **For the rice crust,** put the ghee in a large, round container and whip with your palm till it liquifies.
2. Gradually add the rice flour and salt and knead with your palm into a smooth dough.
3. Divide the dough equally into 2 rounds and place them in a bowl of ice-cold water.

Desserts

4. **For the wholewheat rounds,** combine the semolina, wholewheat flour and salt in a large bowl.
5. Add the water, and knead into a soft dough.
6. Add the rose water and ghee, and knead for 10 more minutes. Divide equally into 2 rounds; keep aside.
7. **For the stuffing,** cook the split red gram in a pressure cooker with 2½ cups of water for about 15 minutes until soft. Transfer into a large vessel and add the sugar, nutmeg-cardamom powder, vanilla essence, 2 tbsp ghee, and black cumin seeds. Mix well.
8. Add the raisins, cherries, and onion seeds and if the red gram is not thick, reheat and cool till it thickens.
9. Spread one of the wholewheat flour rounds onto a flat surface with your fingertips till it becomes circular and is the size of a quarter plate. Then take one ball of the rice crust which was put in water and spread it over the wholewheat flour layer making it into a flat circle roughly 5-6″ in diameter. Similarly make a disc of the second rice flour crust and wholewheat flour round.
10. Divide the red gram mixture into 2 equal portions and place each on the two flattened layers. Fold the layer over the dal and, roll into a ball. Pat the stuffed roll flat with your palm till it is 6″ wide. Repeat with the second round.
11. Heat 1 tbsp ghee on an iron griddle (*tawa*); place one stuffed round carefully in the centre. Cook for 5 minutes on each side shifting it back and forth with 2 pieces of soft cloth till golden brown. Repeat with the second round.
12. Cut into wedges and serve hot with tea.

Sev
Dry vermicelli delight

Preparation time: 10 min.
Cooking time: 30 min.
Serves: 6-8

Ingredients:

Vermicelli (*sev*), roasted	5 cups / 500 gm
Vegetable oil	1 tbsp / 15 ml
Almonds (*badam*), blanched, finely chopped	1 cup / 120 gm
Raisins (*kishmish*), soaked for 30 minutes	1 cup / 100 gm
Sugar	400 gm
Rose water (*gulab jal*)	2 tsp / 10 ml
Green cardamoms (*choti elaichi*), powdered	6
Nutmeg (*jaiphal*) powder	¼ tsp / ½ gm

(Photograph on front cover)

Method:

1. Heat the oil in a pan; add the almonds and raisins; sauté till slightly golden. Remove and drain the excess oil on absorbent paper towels. Keep aside.
2. Now heat 1 tbsp oil in a pan; add the vermicelli and sauté till brown. Add the sugar and ¾ cup water. Mix thoroughly.
3. Cover the pan and cook on low heat till the mixture is dry.
4. If the vermicelli is still not cooked, then sprinkle a bit of water and keep the pan on a griddle and cook for 10-15 minutes more.
5. Transfer contents on a plate, sprinkle rose water, green cardamom powder and nutmeg powder.
6. Serve garnished with fried almonds and raisins.

Rava

Semolina garnished with dried fruits

Preparation time: 10 min.
Cooking time: 30 min.
Serves: 6-8

Desserts

I n g r e d i e n t s :

Semolina (*suji*)	2½ cups / 250 gm
Ghee	1 cup / 190 gm
Almonds (*badam*), blanched	1 cup / 120 gm
Raisins (*kishmish*)	2 cups / 200 gm
Eggs, beaten	4
Milk, full cream, cold	5½ cups / 1 lt
Green cardamoms (*choti elaichi*), powdered	6
Nutmeg (*jaiphal*) powder	¼ tsp / ½ gm
Rose water (*gulab jal*)	2 tsp / 10 ml

M e t h o d :

1. Heat ½ cup ghee in a wok (*kadhai*); fry the almonds and raisins. Remove and drain the excess oil on absorbent paper towels.

2. In the same ghee, add the semolina, sauté on low heat till a pleasant aroma emanates. Then remove and mix in ½ cup water. Return to heat and cook for 2-3 minutes.

3. Remove from heat and add the sugar.

4. Mix the eggs and milk together. Add this to the semolina mixture. Return to heat, cook on a low flame, stirring continuously, to avoid formation of lumps. Add ghee, bit by bit, till the mixture thickens. Mix in the green cardamom powder, nutmeg powder, and rose water.

5. Serve warm in a big bowl, garnished with almonds, raisins and a dash of rose water.

Lagan Nu Custard
Wedding custard

Preparation time: 5 min.
Cooking time: 1 hr.
Serves: 4-6

Desserts

Ingredients:

Milk	4 cups / 720 ml
Sugar	1²/₃ cups / 250 gm
Eggs, beaten	3
Vanilla essence	1 tsp / 5 ml
Rose water (*gulab jal*)	1 tsp / 5 ml
Green cardamom (*choti elaichi*)	
powder	1 tsp / 2 gm
Nutmeg (*jaiphal*), grated	½ tsp / 1 gm
Almonds (*badam*), blanched, sliced	10

Method:

1. Boil the milk and sugar on low heat till it is reduced to half the quantity. Keep aside to cool.
2. Add the eggs, vanilla essence, rose water, and green cardamom powder.
3. Pour the mixture into a baking dish, add the nutmeg and almonds and bake at 350°F / 180°C for 40-50 minutes or till the top is golden brown. Remove from the oven, cool and refrigerate.
4. Cut into pieces and serve

(Photograph on page 4)

Badam Pak
Almond and wholemilk fudge squares

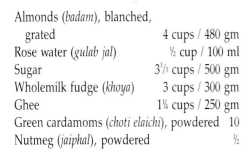

Preparation time: 5 min.
Cooking time: 20 min.
Serves: 6-8

Ingredients:

Almonds (*badam*), blanched, grated	4 cups / 480 gm
Rose water (*gulab jal*)	½ cup / 100 ml
Sugar	3⅓ cups / 500 gm
Wholemilk fudge (*khoya*)	3 cups / 300 gm
Ghee	1¼ cups / 250 gm
Green cardamoms (*choti elaichi*), powdered	10
Nutmeg (*jaiphal*), powdered	½

Method:

1. Boil the rose water and sugar together. Remove from heat after one boil.
2. Add the wholemilk fudge to the rose water syrup and mix thoroughly so that the consistency is smooth. Add the almonds and ghee.
3. Cook on low heat, stirring constantly with a wooden spoon, until the almond mixture leaves the sides of the pan.
4. Add the green cardamom powder and nutmeg powder. Mix well.
5. Spread this mixture on a greased plate.
6. When cool, cut into squares and serve.

Suggested Menus

Non-vegetarian
Lagan Na Chicken Farcha
(*Chicken deep-fried with egg*)   51
Patra Ne Machhi
(*Chutney fish steamed in banana leaves*)   40

or

Vegetarian
Dhansak
(*Mixed grams and vegetables without meat*)   20
Lagansala Stew (*Wedding stew*)   60

Accompaniments
Parsi Biryani
(*Flavoured rice mixed with spicy meat*)   68
Lagan Nu Achar (*Wedding pickle*)   78

Dessert
Lagan Nu Custard   (*Wedding custard*)   90

Non-vegetarian
Sali Ma Murgh (*Chicken with potato straws*)   48
Parsi Gosht Ne Curry
(*Lamb curry flavoured with coconut*)   36

or

Vegetarian
Dhan Dar (*Split red gram tempered with garlic*)   62
Khatu Meethu Stew
(*Sweet and sour vegetable stew*)   58

Accompaniments
Brown Chawal (*Brown cinnamon rice*)   66
Colmi Nu Achar (*Fresh prawn pickle*)   81

Dessert
Rava (*Semolina garnished with dried fruits*)   88

Glossary of Cooking Terms

Batter — A mixture of flour, liquid and sometimes other ingredients, of a thin or thick, creamy consistency.

Blend — To mix together thoroughly two or more ingredients.

Dropping consistency — If a spoonful of mixture is lifted from the bowl, it should drop off the spoon in 5 seconds.

Marinade — To soak meat, fish or vegetable in a mixture of seasoning ingredients to add flavour and to make it tender.

Knead — To work a dough by hand or machine until smooth.

Purée — To press food through a fine sieve or blend it in a blender or food processor to a smooth, thick mixture.

Simmer — To boil gently on low heat.

Steam — Cook by heat or steam. Generally food to be steamed is put in a perforated container which is placed above a pan of boiling water. The food should not come into contact with the water.

Syrup — A concentrated solution of sugar in water.

Index

ISBN: 81-7436-193-6

Second impression 2004
© **Roli & Janssen BV 2002**
Published in India by Roli Books
in arrangement with Roli & Janssen
M 75, Greater Kailash II Market, New Delhi-110 048, India
Tel.: ++91 (011) 29212271, 29212782, Fax: ++91 (011) 29217185
E-mail: roli@vsnl.com, Website: rolibooks.com

Photographs: Sunny Singh

Printed and bound in Singapore